Free Music CD with book purchase.

To receive your free recording of
author Danice Sweet
singing her songs
which she illustrated in this
book,
fill out this coupon and mail it
to the address below.

PLEASE PRINT

Name: _____

Street Address: _____

City, State, Zip Code: _____

MAIL TO:

Pearson Publishing Company
711 N. Carancahua, Suite 119
Corpus Christi, Texas 78475

Written and Illustrated
By
Danice E. Sweet

2006

Pearson Publishing Company
Corpus Christi

Copyright © 2006 by Danice E. Sweet

All rights reserved. No part of this book may be reproduced or transmitted in any form or by any means, electronic or mechanical, including photocopy, recording, or any information and storage and retrieval system, without prior written permission from the publisher, except by a reviewer who may quote brief passages in a review.

Library of Congress Control Number: 2006939113

ISBN-13: 978-0-9768083-8-1, paperback
ISBN-10: 0-9768083-8-2, paperback

Cover art: Danice E. Sweet
Cover production: Tamara Schleman of Graphics, Etc.
Book design: Katherine Pearson Jagoe Massey
Music notation: Terry Lewis

Published by
Pearson Publishing Company
Corpus Christi, Texas
www.PearsonPub.US

This book
is lovingly dedicated
to my mother,
Gloria Clover,
for encouraging me to draw,
even in church.

Thanks to my sister, Dayna Beaty,
for the idea of combining
my love for music
and my love for art.

A special thank you
to my incredibly great nephew
Gabriel,
who makes me smile
every single day
of my life.

And to our very own Noah.
May your faith in God be strengthened
each time you see
a rainbow.

Danice Sweet

Bible Stories

In

Songs and Pictures

Table of Contents

Floating Zoo

from the

Holy Bible
Book of Genesis
Chapters 6 - 9

Page 1

Whale Motel

from the

Holy Bible
Book of Jonah
Chapters 1 - 2

Page 43

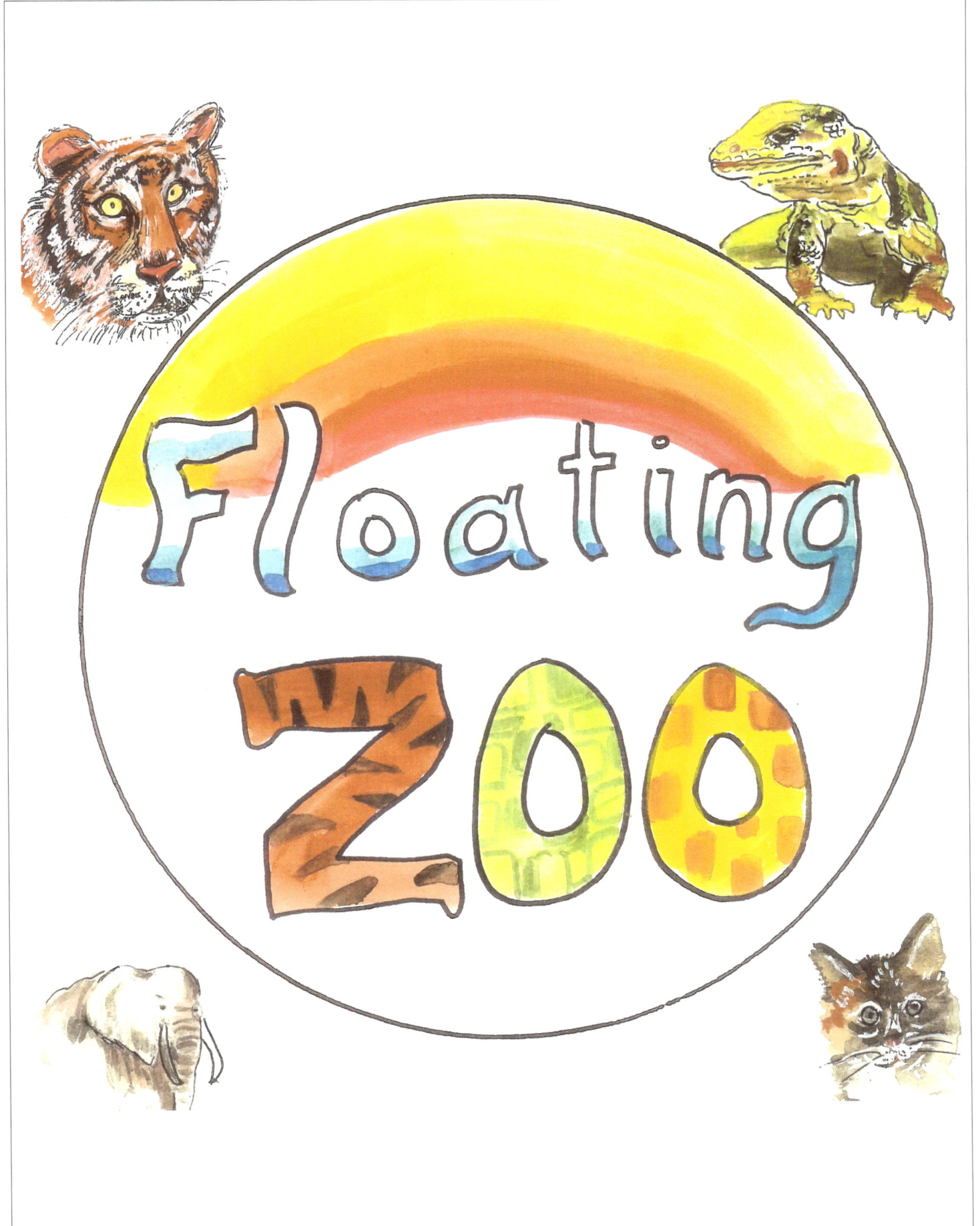

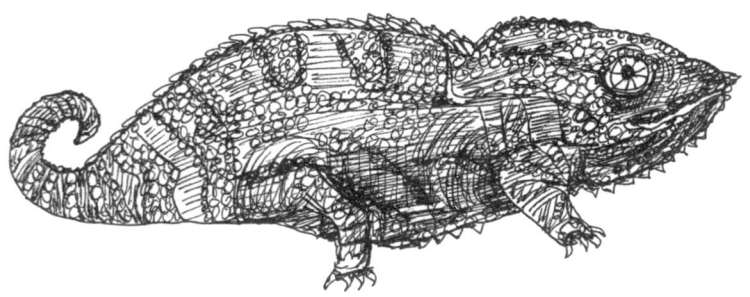

A man named Noah
started building a big boat.

He didn't know whether
that gopher bark would float.

But when the Lord says "jump"
you do what you must do.

So Noah made the very first floating zoo!

When the waves started rockin,'
the ostriches squawkin,'
there was no way to hide in the sand.

The elephants wondered,
with all that thunder,
would this ship ever hit land?

But forty days later,
all the alligators,
and the other creatures
two by two,

Well, they opened the door,
and thanked the Lord
for the very first
floating zoo.

Well, the neighbors laughed
at the cruise ship in the yard.

And the smell those creatures left made living hard.

When it started to pour,
they all stood there in shock.

But God shut the door,
and that sea cruise
started to rock.

When the waves started rockin,'
the ostriches squawkin,'
there was no way to hide in the sand.

The elephants wondered,
with all that thunder,
would this ship ever hit land?

Well, forty days later,
all the alligators,
and the other creatures
two by two,

Well, they opened the door,
and they thanked the Lord
for the very first
floating zoo!

So when the rainbow shines
just remember the time,
and thank the Lord
you knew

Old Noah
was a floatin,'

About the great big ark
that played a part
in the very first
floating zoo!

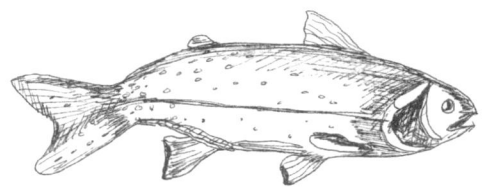
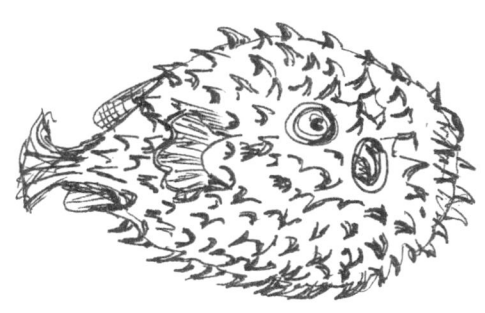
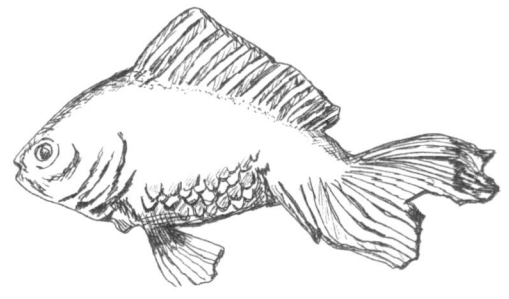

It was a Whale Motel
not even with a view.
It was really just a pit.

After a three day stay,
a prayin' night and day,
Jehovah made the big fish spit!

The sea was getting rougher,
and the sailors started sweating,
but they didn't want poor Jonah
to get wet.

Jonah kept insisting that the sea
would stop its waving
if they'd throw him in
without a single net.

After crying to the Father,
praying to Him in the water,
the sailors put poor Jonah overboard.

Fearing for their innocence,
they sacrificed in self defense,
and seafood was provided by the Lord.

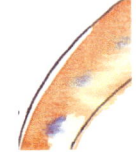

The first devotional
where Jonah prayed
was inside the catch of the day.

It was a Whale Motel
not even with a view.
It was really
just a pit.

After a three day stay
a praying night and day,

Jehovah made the
big fish spit!

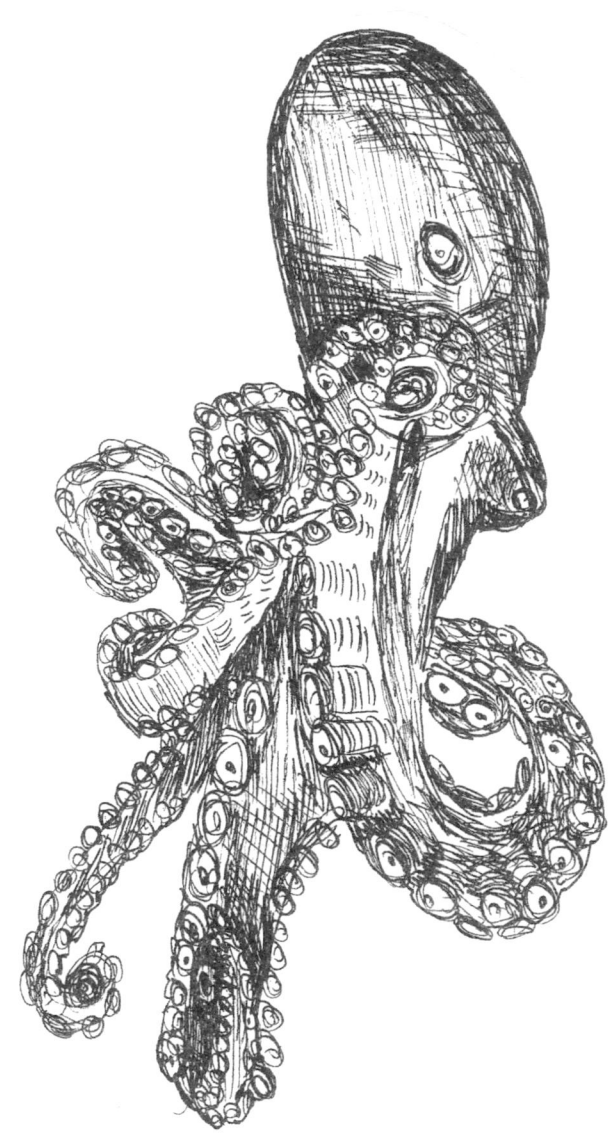

Danice Sweet

is an author, illustrator, songwriter and painter. After the
encouragement of family and friends, she decided to
combine her talents and create this illustrated children's book on the
Floating Zoo and the Whale Motel.
Both stories are songs she wrote many years ago.

Danice is giving a CD of these original songs to
purchasers of this book.
The CD was recorded by her group Revival
and another group, Revelation.
To obtain a copy of the CD fill out and mail in the coupon in the front
of this book.

For more information about Revival's music you can locate their website
at www.revivalministry.us.
Revival has recorded eleven projects and has traveled throughout the
United States, Canada and Ukraine
for the past sixteen years.

Danice has been a public school art
instructor for the past seventeen years.

The original illustrations for this book are watercolor on
watercolor paper and pen and ink.

December 2006

PEARSON PUBLISHING COMPANY
CORPUS CHRISTI, TEXAS

For a complete list and description of our publications and to order books, please go to our website:

www.PearsonPub.US

Catching the Dream: A Parent's Guide to Children's Dreams
    By Janet S. Gould $26.95

Deal Me In
    By Alyce Guynn with illustrations by Jesse Taylor $23.95

His Angels Are In Charge
    By Frances Cotten Woodard $24.95

Beyond These Eyes
    By Nicole Niewoehner

The Sacred Gifts
    By Katherine Jagoe Massey

Slumbertime: A Parent's Guide for Children's Sleep and Sleep Problems
    By Janet S. Gould

Whale Motel and the Floating Zoo
    By Danice Sweet $26.95

For pricing go to our website.

To mail in orders, send (1) a list of titles with number of copies of each title, (2) check or money order for total retail price of all books, plus (3) $5.00 shipping and handling for each book, and (4) your name and mailing address printed clearly, to:

Pearson Publishing Company
711 N. Carancahua, Suite 119
Corpus Christi, Texas 78475

www.ingramcontent.com/pod-product-compliance
Ingram Content Group UK Ltd.
Pitfield, Milton Keynes, MK11 3LW, UK
UKHW061139180426
11947UKWH00002B/12